AIRY HALL

Leiceste

By the same author
Mama Dot

AIRY HALL

Fred D'Aguiar

Chatto & Windus
LONDON

Published in 1989 by
Chatto & Windus Ltd
30 Bedford Square
London WC1B 3SG

A CIP catalogue record for this book is available
from the the British Library.

ISBN 0 7011 3340 6

Phototypeset by Rowland Phototypesetting Ltd
Printed in Great Britain by
Redwood Burn Ltd
Trowbridge, Wiltshire

ACKNOWLEDGEMENTS
Acknowledgements and thanks are due to the editors of
the following publications in which some of these poems
first appeared: *First and Always* (Faber), *Kunapipi*,
The Poetry Book Society Anthology 1985, and *1986/87*,
Poetry Review, *Race Today*, *Soho Square*
(Bloomsbury), *Stand*.

CONTENTS

In memory of Malcolm D'Aguiar
1935–1987

PART ONE

Airy Hall

The red sand road, houses well back,
Trees there to collect dust
Whipped by traffic and flung at them,
The log bridge I am forever crossing
For a sound logs make as they shuffle
Underfoot, the lop-sided main gate
That has to be lifted into place,
Palings you can swing up and duck
Sideways through if loose and if known,
Tsetse flies stickled on their spikes
We take all afternoon approaching,
Just to pincer the papery tails
Between the thumb and index fingers:
How many pushed off those tips
Leaving us all open and mannered,
As I am left now, now and always.

Airy Hall, First Light

When asleep, my back
To Airy Hall's first light,
Every corner faced takes
A mirror's silvered edge
Flashed and flashed at me.

When I fasten my lids,
A thick dark is punctured
By stars; when I surrender
The stars become flowers;
When the flowers are thrown

They sprout doves,
Doves that arc fluently
Back to my clasp:
Star, flower and dove,
Bring me the light I love.

Airy Hall Barrier

Many deny what we see
Has anything to do with anything:
The imperialist who will not let us forget;
The runner crossing the city ahead of taxis;
Fireflies whose phosphorus belongs everywhere.

I follow the sound to a door,
One that opens on approach
To my room in water,
Pooled and swirling as if plunged
From a falls: Kaiteur.

Water sounding again,
This time a cliff-face,
Scaffold and men blasting rock
To the year of nought;
Somehow the sonic genius of a bat,

To stay latched to that sound
And find the true falls.

Airy Hall Wash-Day

Linen beaten outdoors
On wooden slabs with wood-paddles:
Those nothing else hours.

Smaller things are ducked
In soapy water, scrubbing at a slant,
The whole weight behind ribbed board and tub.

Niftier ones are gripped in both hands, wrung —
There is a consonant squelch as soap
Shoots out with grime.

I see her straighten and toss what's done
In a basin for hanging . . . a circuit
Of sagged washlines, our separates dripped

All pruned and leaden;
Inscrutably sun-buffed, wind-buffed,
They finish chattering on the line.

I'd shadow her, palms ready for her okay,
Feeling her eye for detail on me from my sprint
To my emergency stop at the blinding line.

Piled to eye-level I loved to lean my head
On such heat; their no-scent smell;
Pigeon-stepping back to the house in her arms.

Airy Hall, Mid-Morning

Sun liquefies
Reinforced glass,
Even allowing for refraction,
The staggering effect of blinds,
Mesmerising fans and soft drinks,
Bakes to discolorations
You and your things.

Someone revs a tractor
Left idle or turning over long;
Fumes take time to ride the stillness;
The incense stick you burn
Hoping to drown them is strong,
A strength that wrestles free
The volley of sneezes you must do,

Never one or two.
All this at the lights through amber,
Green and amber again,
Rapt in last night's talk
Which grew into sweeter things:
Waking still inside her and she woken
As you withdraw and roll on your side.

Airy Hall Iconography

The Tamarind hangs its head,
stings the eyes with its breath.

The Mango traps the sun by degrees,
transforms its rays into ambrosia.

The Coconut's perfect seal lets in rain,
bends with solid milk and honey.

The Guava is its own harvest,
each seed bound in fleshy juice.

The Guinep's translucence is all yours
if you skin its lips, chew its seed for the raw.

The Stinking-toe might be lopped off a stale foot,
on the tongue it does an about-turn: myrrh.

The Paw-paw runs a feather along your nose,
you want it to stop, you want more.

The Sour-sop's veneer is the wasp
treading air at the vaulted honeycomb.

The Sapodilla ducks you twice in frankincense,
you are fished out fighting to go down a third time.

Airy Hall's Dynasty

The house added to wing by wing
Has lost its symmetry. Marriages
Under the one roof are an upward
Curve. Children count from great-
Grandchildren in dozens, half-dozens,
Not twos or threes. Paint on wood
Go back to another age, one
Sewn up inside the pitch a gas-lamp,
Signing arms and voices map.

    Boundaries you had to respect,
    Fictions you now inspect.

So many layers has the wood spongy,
A feel you double-take every time.
To restore banisters and stairs,
You move through captured rainbows
Picking up sheer grain at last.
Brace yourself for the names;
Eraser, not restorer; rubbing out
Your own thumbprint and the dead's
Defenceless save your belief in ghosts.

    Boundaries you had to respect,
    Fictions you now inspect.

Later, you examine your thumbs,
Naked, you'd clothe them in those
Several layers against the years:
A first brushstroke steered by
Your guide's steady pressure,
Your hand in his, fleshy and warm.
A direction you learn, then resist,
Resisting until it lets you go,
To find a groove all yours.

    Boundaries you had to respect,
    Fictions you now inspect.

Airy Hall's Feathered Glories

Birds the ambitious among us trap.
We spend life hearing songs from this one,
Boasts from that; sticks, sticks, sticks,
At inviting angles, covered in gum
These bird-catchers chew till jaws ache,
Mixed with something bled from trees.

They hide, sights on the planted sticks;
We mill, one stork-foot against our lean;
All track as best they can a bird's pelt
Across the open: an impossible curve,
Dead stops in thin air, about turns,
Pirouettes, spinning our heads.

As a bird lands we see its changes.
From surprise anchored in stillness –
A stillness buoyed by such quiet,
A quiet of knowing what's what –
To wing-beats, loose feathers,
Cries that make us stop our ears,

Look away or clamp eyelids. Inside,
The last lighted image: a stick
Swaying with capture, fuelling,
Refuelling; a gum taste far back
On the upper palate and a song
Singled out from scores in an aviary.

After an absence hard to string
A sentence in, ambition itself,
Nursed from crawl, to walk, to run,
Enters the brashest of suns, cages
Held high as lamps, mirrors or trophies
Brimming a tongue-tied, granite dark.

Airy Hall's Common Denominators

The road's equatorial run
Through Airy Hall;
Houses, whitewashed or mud-daubed,
Blinded by trees that catch sand
Before the grains lodge in slatted windows;
A trench, parched or flooded,
Bleached or submarine,
According to one of two seasons.

Add a solitary donkey
Braying at midday the moment its harness
Lifts away for lunch; its short trot
And hind-legs-buck as it settles to graze;
A crow to peck puffed-up ticks
Rosy-mouthed and leathery.

Rice someone sat and picked clean
All morning on the verandah has swelled,
Full as the sifted flour is brown;
A stew gurgles and will hold its readiness
For the rest of the day if necessary —

It is hardly necessary;
You scrape your bare feet on the matting,
Push past the swinging half-doors
Hat in hand, blinking in the halved light.

Airy Hall Ward

There will be days when you or I are bedridden,
Unable to stomach direct light or a voice.
Who fly-posts town?
Word spreads faster than the virus
Rusting the joints; weeks' worth of picked fruit
Turns the whole place into an orchard.

It's enough to make anyone get up.
All this loving and understanding
That's just there for when
You're in a bad way
And all the time I'm thinking
They must have the wrong address altogether:

The door-knocker that had to be silenced
With a bandage, the children shooed
From the sick part of the house –
Partitioned, horticulturally sound,
And a solid stillness
You had to whisper in and labour through.

Airy Hall Autumn

A gust flips
the white undersides
of leaves
to the light.
Some loosen,
describe a slowed,
ziggurat fall.

We dash one way,
jab air another
to catch any.
Most grip a thick dark,
framing in mid-air
the four corners
of stars stared at.

For the feel
as their dry spines
crumble in your moist palm —
its kept warmth,
veined as a new leaf,
keeping all seasons —
grab, be airborne and grab.

Airy Hall's Exits

Salt over the shoulder
Or a trip curtailed,
On account of the black cat
That crossed your path.

Last rites for the sick
In a house a crow
Overflew or preened itself on
And cawed, cawed, cawed.

A black dress, the gift
From a relative you've never seen,
For the funeral of a friend
You never imagined could die.

The dream you fall in,
Waking seconds before you land,
Your heart backfiring; the dream
You one day fail to wake from.

Airy Hall's Dark Age

Someone's, 'The child is a cross,
He has bad blood through and through,'
Is picked up and amplified across fields.

These vocals stick somehow in the acres
This town covers, against a gale
On its way to tearing up islands.

A child doing the things
Children do: sly, brash, fidgety,
Becomes aligned with the devil.

All that remains is for one among us
To fetch the pint-sized stake
Dressed in razor-grass and bramble.

No sooner the child is ambushed,
An empty paddy-bag he raced in
Swooped over his head and tied,

Rough-shod about waist level,
A lasso from a hand he looked up to
And he is beyond us all.

Airy Hall Rain

Fat, roomy, dust-raising drops,
Close ranks and wall up space:
Steady rain for days. . . .

A lullaby, it sends us off early;
Or huddled, our voices low,
Up to our necks in bedding.

We hear of lost bridges,
Holes where a road should be,
A house on stilts turned ark.

Before the mustiness and absence,
Some of us will lose friends,
Wondering about insects and birds

That must hide and feed somewhere;
Forgetting the rain like a heart,
Pulsed and faltering when a beat misses.

Airy Hall at Night

1

Moonlight cushions thought,
Rounds the hard edge of fence
Gate and tarpaulin, brings the pond
At the bottom of the yard
To the swinging half-doors
You duck through
As light wades into darknesses;
A counter-flap you lift
Turning 180° to face where you came,
Lowered with a strangled thud.

2

A night without stars, moon or lamplight,
Lowers heads in its tent;
Flaps drawn at the corners and pegged
To moistening ground. Accept
If you walk for long enough
You'd hit a wall that gives a little
Before gathering itself
To send you reeling back.
Now the insects' clatter makes sense,
It is time to leave.

3

If you step on a toad,
You will know you have stepped on a toad.
You cannot forget what you have done.
You wash your foot, towel it,
And still feel the trodden toad
Underfoot: how you jumped higher
Than any toad, using the toad's back
As a trampoline; how it worked as one,
Though sunk inches into dry earth
Bouncing out of sight as if a finger

Had pushed it, head and body down,
Not a foot stepped on its back.
We see them ride each other for hours,
Motionless or dragging their bellies
Over fields to a secluded spot;
Fill their necks like trumpet players
And blast the night open; we see all this
Remembering the exact pressure of frogs
On our soles. We shake heads to clear them;
The frogs stick as if rooted there.

Airy Hall Isotope

Consider our man in a hovel
With no windows, a shack our missiles
Sail through; cracks that do not interrupt
The flow of moonlight or sunlight,
Seen here washing or baking his floor.

Consider too, our woman, reputed to fly
At night on the very broom that sweeps
Her yard printless; the same broom
Used to swipe Dog eyeing Hen's egg,
Noisily announced by Hen, drooled over
By Dog that is hungry, hungry;
Dreaming the one dream starring Hen.

Consider last, any boy convalescing
In a house crucified between those two
(How he was among the first to fling
Sand stones), spreadeagled
In her mud hut, she massages him
After two days in a pain she alone
Kills with her curious touch.

Consider these and you have a life,
Several lives lapping the one sun,
Casting the same lengthening shadows
From a moon so strapping, the children
Play bat and ball and make clean catches.

Airy Hall Nightmare

You sleep little and light
In a bed made for two big people.
Now the springs are brands;
Now electric rings;
Now nails stacked close as bristles.

You are in this bed on the open sea
Strapped under bedding tucked in tight,
Without the strength to lift your arm,
The one with a thousand needles
Or stripped of all nerves, it's not yours.

Nose down in a pillow,
How can you shift the boulder
That is your likeness,
Greying by the second?
With sheer will? How indeed.

Airy Hall Leave-Taking

Talk about leaving Airy Hall
Remains just that – talk.
Down to the last man to disappear
Round the bend from Airy Hall.

A town turned out to watch
His broad back rhythmically tot up
Almost obsolete yards between his past
And a future he erased with each blind step.

His name was a buzz, then a hum,
Then hardly a breath.
Now it is an absence,
The best of us could not fill.

His was the shadow of the man that left,
Found in a kennel owned by
The mangy dog he threw scraps at
When he was someone:

We forget his name; we think we hear
A man yelp where a dog should be;
Who can be sure at this late hour
Or ever.

PART TWO

The Cow *Perseverance*

I

Here I am writing you on old newspaper against a tide of
    print,

In the regular spaces between lines (there are no more
    trees).

I've turned it upside-down to widen the gap bordering
    sense and nonsense,

For what I must say might very well sound as if it were
    topsy-turvy.

I put myself in your shoes (unable to recall when I last set
    eyes on a pair).

You read everything twice, then to be doubly sure, aloud,

Testing their soundness: *we wash cow's dung for its grain,*

And I feel your stomach turn; it's not much unlike
    collecting it for fuel,

Or mixed with clay to daub cracks in our shelters and
    renew door-mounds

That free us of rain, insects and spirits. They no longer
    drop the milk

We let them live for; their nights spent indoors for safe
    keep,

Their days tethered to a nearby post. People eye them so,
    they are fast

Becoming our cross; you'd think they'd fallen out of the
    sky.

II

Hunger has filled them with what I can only call
    compassion.
Such bulbous, watery eyes blame us for the lack of grass
    and worse,
Expect us to do something; tails that held the edge of
    windscreen wipers
In better days, swishing the merest irritant, a feather's
    even,
Let flies congregate until the stretched, pockmarked hide is
    them.
That's why, when you asked how things were, I didn't have
    to look far,
I thought, *Let the cow explain, its leathery tongue has run
    this geography*
Many times over; how milk turns, unseen, all at once, so
    lush pastures
Threw up savannahs. The storms are pure dust or deep
    inside the rowdiest
Among us, virtually dead and rowdy because they know it,
    they're not sure
What else to do. You fathom why, when a cow croons, we
    offer it
What we can't as a bribe for it to stop: *silence is
    perseverance.*

III

We watch its wait on meagre haunches, ruminating on
  what must be
Imperishable leather, some secret mantra, our dear
  buddha, for the miracle
We need; and us, with nowhere to turn, find we believe.
  God knows
It's a case of choosing which pot-hole in the road to ride;
  knowing
We export the asphalt that could fill them; knowing too
  the one thing
We make these days that is expressly ours is whipped in
  malarial water
And forced down our throats for daring to open our
  mouths.
Give us the cow's complicity anyday: its perfect art of
  being left
In peace; its till-now effortless conversion of chewy grass
  to milk;
And its daft hoof-print, ignored for so long though clearly
  trespassing.
Then and then alone, we too can jump over the moon,
  without bloodshed.
Its raised-head and craned-neck attempt to furnish an
  exact account
Is a tale you and I are bound to finish, in flesh or spirit.

El Dorado Update

Riddle me, riddle me, riddle.
One people, one nation, one destiny?
   Let's take a walk
   not to stay, just to see.

You pass a man at Customs,
returning from an island;
he wears several tin chains,
tin rings on every finger,
and tin bracelets that jingle
as his arms swing.

Customs ensure
what he declares
tallies with their list made
when he departed
with identical amounts
of gold.

You know his jaunt by heart:
   The stricter the government,
   the wiser the population.

Riddle me, riddle me, riddle.
In an overloaded taxi, you are warned
not to lean against the door
that is not a door; you spend your journey
keeping your feet out of gaps in the floor;
you share a begging bowl with children and ministers;
what coins you earn are only good for wells.

To pass the betting shop you must cross the road;
people congregate from opening time to close;
they place the day's meal from pawned things
on a favourite or outsider and pray it will multiply;
they throw hands in a partner:

> They are you and I
> forced to take the reflection
> in the puddle for sky.

> *Riddle me, riddle me, riddle.*
Big business has pulled out overnight:
houses left to servants, shops to cockroaches.
You separate the twin-ply of toilet rolls,
pinch grammes off every measurement
and spread your goods on the floor
for the morning's trade
in a sheet you can fold quick.

Broken bones cannot be set;
simple wounds go septic.
It's back to losing toe-nails
on stony roads.

> *Back to back, belly to belly,*
> *we don't give a damn,*
> *we done dead already.*

You think it's easy?
You walk down the middle
of the road with your head
in the air.

Crowd on the left-hand side shout,
'Stop for something to eat, no?
Wheat-flour scarce,
rice-flour is eye-pass,
we got cassava bread,
mauby and class.'

Crowd on the right side
play a different tune,
they point smoking guns,
they say, 'All eat rice,
that is revolutionary food,
don't bother with wheat import,
imperialist food;
we're the proprietor of this country,
not the administrator.'

    Riddle me, riddle me, riddle.
You get choke-and-rob,
call the police;
you don't know in the dark
you can't tell Jack from Jill;
you say 'I'm Indian,
the deed was done by an African';
they show you an identity parade
full of Indians;
they're going to charge you
for wasting precious time,
if you don't leave their station.

You think it's easy?
Police don't have radio, nor hook;
they can't catch crook by telepathy,
much less get from A to B.
Their ink-well run dry
so they can't take your statement;
plus they're busy, bad bad bad,
capturing smuggler,
possessor of garlic, onion,
wheat-flour, and trade union sympathiser.

It's true; it's cheaper to get convicted
for possession of marijuana than bread;
they spot-check schoolchildren's packed lunches
for bake; they raid weddings and seize
roti and cake.

Lord, what to do in this fowl-coop
republic, risk my neck on a demo
or in a food queue?

    Let's take a walk
      not to stay, just to see.
What people, what nation, what destiny?
    Riddle me, riddle me, riddle.

Only The President's Eggs are Yellow

Everyone else's resembles
Condensed milk; 'sunny-side up'
Offered as a snipe alternative.

All desires boil down to a visa,
A queue, longer than the electorate,
Half the national football team
Jumped, disappearing on tour.

The electric grid scrimps at half-strength.
Videos wait, doubling as bases for plants;
Televisions reflect exactly what is around them;
Fridges like empty coffins have a wise patience,
Keeping stale air stale at sauna-temperature.

A hundred-year tree the country's new main road
Circumnavigated either side to pass,
Spontaneously uprooted; my first cousin
Planted a nimble offshoot in its place;
In a tropics where the rains are simply due,
Its youth showed, wilting in the heat.

This democracy is forced-ripe, for what?
You can tell by how newer and newer conscripts
Dismiss being dunked, feet-up in water-barrels;
How they carry themselves as if smelling
Responsibilities far above their stations;
How they dash grudging salutes at civilians
Earmarked for nursed rounds of ammunition

(Bursting with too much importance to notice).
The American Embassy tends all their street's
Litter and trees, painted in brilliant stockings;
Shutters angled to see out, not in;
A private generator to cook cold air and ice.
I had to crawl for a visa to enter the country;

Not because I'm an undesirable, it's unwritten
Policy in line with giant economies.
A clerk supplements a low salary anyhow;
Washing one shirt every night; without
Deodorants, a skunk an hour into the day.

A strapping man, about my age, with bare feet
Begged me for any loose change I could spare.
I emptied all the tinny noise in my pockets
Into his cupped hands: 'Thanks, English.'

By twelve o'clock egg and sun look alike:
Whole office blocks are warped L.P.s;
A gross tremor threatening the real.

Earth

In the end we come to you prostrated.

We bear a black mark on our foreheads,
Once the Muezzin's preserve.

You open for our entry clean as a dive
Whose rings — a trunk's year's stockpile —
Are all the pool widens.

Stone and Shell

I used a stone to pound a shell;
I pounded it to smithereens,
Then ground it into dust.

Now the shell is hushed;
I weigh the stone against the dust.

Frontline Chronicle

I

Our differences loomed large as airships
A stone's throw high: 'Whatever you say
Must be said direct, no embroidery,
No honeying the facts to make them palatable.'
He pushed bodily from the table,
His weight grating the chair on the boards.
I was nailed there, my blood rising, feeling
A faint shudder I tried to fight worsen.

I shouted at the door, 'You don't know.'
As a girl granny saw her first blimp
Fill the sky over her and stoned it.
'What does that mean?' I don't know.
If you were her age you were fighting
For cover, not out arming yourself.

II

When other towns died, ours buzzed.
Food we associated with home choked its air.
The one break from our eyeball to eyeball
Was for paper plates heaped and steaming:
Lashings of pepper, mouth water, sarsaparilla
To wash it down; 'Man can't think on hungry belly.'
The best smoke came after we caned the meal,
A lull that picked up full throttle.

We emerged to frosted cars and the uniform dark
Time-locked houses entertained; our long goodbyes
Reverberated. During the hop-in, hop-out drive
Or springy steps home, it could have been any
They pulled beside and bundled into the van
You'd be carried from, into the station, dead.

A Great House by the Sea

The routine jab
becomes a form of torture.
A door held for someone
important, too long,
loses its perfumed environment
for one fumigated.

One man dies,
another steps into his shoes;
a mother's final cry
begins her child's.

This house is big enough
for us to stay lonely.
There are books to outlast life,
rooms for a small drama,
an invited audience,
and a scullery, marble table *in situ*.

Our first smell of the sea
is dead flesh we mistake
for poisonous farts;
this night air is shitty.
We race indoors for body odour,
for air fired by central heating.
Our voices carry so well
it takes for ever to find ourselves.

I Buried My Father a Complete Stranger

One close day in E5 or E6, the mute hearse
rounded the corner and filled his street.

At the parlour I looked and looked
at the boy asleep. I could have kissed him
on his brow with every hair in place or wept.

We stood by empty seats shifting our weight,
drove deliberately to a hole made for him,
buried the child and took the man away.

Spirit-Level

I've not seen a sky like it since:
A heavy blue, except for a flame's fringe.

I searched it for the usual shapes
That shift from one known thing to another.

It gave nothing of itself save this blue,
Lightening; reddened at the heart

Of something. As a medical team waits
On the first aquamarine spike

From a wired cardiac arrest, so I braced
For this build-up, its every colourful trapping

Moulted to touch I'm not sure what.
Any sign of a quickening in me would do.

Thank goodness my life didn't depend on it.
There I was, stuck till a cramp set in,

Seeing chimneys begin their long exhalations
In that drifting place between roof and sky —

Passing too easily as cloud — and spires
Trained on some target exactly beyond.

As if I'd been asleep on my feet, a light
I couldn't look at direct made me jump:

Providing I steered clear of names
Gift-wrapped for me, it might always climb.

PART THREE

The Kitchen Bitch

Note: The Kitchen Bitch, a three-tiered tin lamp with a handle, fuelled by kerosene oil, for many years provided light for Jamaican peasants who could not afford the more sophisticated lamps. (From *Jamaica Journal*)
'Dis a ongle di grigri; di gragra deh behine.'

Jamaican Creole proverb

Prologue
Our man, still in a dream, enters Town
To 50,000 gulls shrieking as they surf
Wind-currents herded to these shores,
In time to catch all the orange lamps
On High Street killed in synchrony,
A first car treading bitumen, its lights
Usual pinpoints dilated to equal blurs,
And dawn charged bright as an albino,
Raising a sun gathered by magnifying lens.

His earliness makes him Man on this hill
Overshadowing Old Town and older sea.
Light frog-leaps border patrols,
Dummy-rolls between their paces,
Returns such edge to fence and steeple.
At this very moment the dream,
Starring trees, begins its late run:
Him falling as a droplet condensed
Off a leaf, exaggeratedly;

Except he lands bad, bounces twice,
Appears added, like one leaf, that drop
Made overnight and dung a bird
Faltering in sea-air releases to earth,
Earth blind until now to any light
He brings. His spread fingers move
Through bars X-raying every vein
In his hand, his flesh grows to possess
A solid dark and cool recoiling from him.

I

Politics: a Hydra-headed Trojan horse,
A one-horse race, those I trusted said.
I took what I had to take or die,
Executed things in politics' name;
Turned out I backed the wrong horse;
Head ate head until there were no heads
Left over what I considered small fry;
Another horse reared up, now I'm framed.
I've come too far to finish in a hearse
Draped with a flag I burnt for street cred.
The umpteenth party for me to guide
(Another day chalked-up in the living game).
Their walking-boots fresh from stores —
You can eat off the perfect tread,
Will grate down to each stepping style
On miles, long, hard and untamed.

2

We're at the mouth, I like to stress,
We're on a living thing for sure.
Left, enough trail to break-in hide
Reflecting you, reflecting on it
(Let's not pretend, this part is best
To those who love an easy ramble), before
We labour deep and below to inside
This valley, this hibernating giant
On our right among those trees:
A thatched ceiling light has to bore
Through Siamese twins joined at the side,
To end up filtered to a green tint
You'll see in there and nowhere else.
Picture you twelve as one body and soul,
Your five senses and a sixth few describe,
At the mercy of this blinding gradient.

3

As we gain on cloud, this bitumen road
You stamp for warmth becomes a miniature
Haircrack, a scrawl, then kapooch,
Nothing: a trip-wire, we drag our feet
To trigger, for a cooked smell, a gourd
Soaking up light, ounce by particular
Ounce. Time thickens sounds double Dutch:
It's a radio silence I like to keep,
Holding out on the outside world;
Illness or accident is its puncture.
You shake heads, an ulcer sits for such
An occasion as this to use as dry peat
Your stomach's rubber sack. Forward
At your pace to where the chalk linear
Fades to unadulterated granite and stick;
Relish the pure, unrefracted heat.

4

They can't wait to muddy those boots.
They slow to an aimlessness to scoff
Their rations, they cross-thread
The screw-on tops of water bottles.
They've no mind for the day's route.
A couple of stragglers, looking tough.
Two loners. Some wanting to be breast-fed
They're so close, engaging me in idle
Talk of past conquests. Valleys are truths
They say and I bite my tongue with a thought:
A thumbprint, one in all the world's dead,
If it's like anything, it's nothing. Rattled,
I kick at my walk-pace which shuts
Them up as they gasp; my quiet laugh.
I manoeuvre to the back of their heads
Eavesdropping on places they've settled;

5

Capitals where they have to plant
New trees, having registered lampposts,
How many traffic lights and zebra
—One comes from a county with three—
Crossings; things I miss. They rant
About me as if I wasn't there; a ghost
I am supposed to fear, or penumbra;
The ghost I came here to bury.
It's me in stories that are ignorant
Versions handed down, line past
Line, to become reduced to the algebra
For any tale, an excursion far from me.
In my wicked moments I'd think,
Quake in your air-cushioned boots,
I am he: what to do with such alfalfa
If it comes from the star in their story?

6

Miles from the bitumen-road they might
Or might not find alone, with fools
Among them seeing a bounty, not a guide;
Heads jammed with floppy facts, not my tale.
Scrap that, do what you're paid night
And day to do: trail-leader for a whole
Week's pay in twenty-four hours; work I tried
Elsewhere for a pittance and failed.
I count my blessings pure as anthracite:
The last to entertain Republican goals.
The stream at last, far below, hidden
By trees and cacophonously male:
A roar that's so even, I get a fright
By the way its loudness is pooled;
The sound of the sea nowhere near seaside;
A sea-sound going up and down the scales.

7

As chalk-gradient bites we see sweat.
Talk lessens to words in a ration.
Clothes tucked in neat as neat can be,
Flap in wind slalomed off a ridge
That is a neck, wind that is a breath.
We'll round a bend to the bald cranium;
Plenty of anything, even if it's free,
Can kill: thin oxygen too hard to average
Causes heartburn; I see my own death.
I see it on this giant plopped on his bum;
Trees are hairs thickest on his body,
Sloping to a point a hand shields;
A place the biggest and the best
Among us cover with a shame we slalom
Through each generation failing to see
Where it's from or why we use it as a bridge.

8

His spread feet outdistance our eyes.
We can't stop up here over long,
Heads spin, sight begins to swim,
Something in me makes me think
Jump with every inkling from this high
It would be my last. I've felt it alone,
How I kept my feet on the hill to win
Is for another to tell; with a squint
I did what leaping was and got by,
Waking to a wind poking me in my bones.
They leap to my order to move off him;
Shutters rattle like traps to print
Everything: negatives that will lie
Exactly as the lies made up along
The way about me and friends close as kin,
Lies transferred into facts that stink.

9

They're accustomed to walk in twos,
Or threes, rarely singly. At times
We could have linked arms and can-canned.
From here on in it's single file.
Sometimes a path, wide as shoes,
Inched along sideways and sometimes
No path at all. Tell them that and
Their sweet trust will turn to bile.
The leaflet did not promise a cruise,
It got them here using the very lines
They use: snaps they can't land
Fast enough, snapping everything while
Nothing gets into every film they choose.
Next we are to descend into pines.
As soon as we're off the head of this man
Couldn't be sooner; on him I am a child.

10

Four to go and we're all of us
On stone steps hands must have lugged
This far. Trampling has gnawed across
The middle of each slab, the ends smeared
With weather, the lubricating stuff
That hovercrafts a snail or slug,
And a tight olive girdle of moss.
My handbook tells me count heads here.
The fool who wrote these rules must
Have stickled in mid-air, in a metal bug,
Getting no closer than the criss-cross
Swing a helicopter's blades can bear
Without clipping the Christmas
Tree tops, thinking this as smug
A spot as any for me to play big-boss
Counting heads and checking all the gear.

11

The stream, here quiet and narrow;
Dark stones with the contours water maps,
Ideal for skipping. My eyes are lazy,
They skipped or sunk two into one;
I fly up and down grown men in a row
Ending with the same bare fact,
The giant's claimed one as his baby.
My, *Which sleepy head's fallen
Behind*, sends eleven heads akimbo,
To that peak where the last four sat
Or stood; the four minus one Mr Sleepy.
That blasted peak! My troubles have begun.
In my scramble for it, I am followed
By two of them, knocking off a few hats
On our way. Not a sign. His name and d.o.b.,
I'll verify; his looks, well, a person

12

I never forget: a stetson-shaded face;
An imperceptible nod like it was afternoon,
Not first thing (still on his first dream);
An uneasiness to start, like everyone.
Albert Collier at the top of my voice
Returns a dozen noms de plume,
Each rebound losing half its steam
As my noise obeys a maths theorem.
In untold trips since my armistice,
The one diabetic I get in a blue moon
Lost his insulin and had to leave the team,
Begging me to reverse my decision,
Against rules made in some office.
Why do we comply? Instinct's an heirloom
I swear by and my army-issue gabardine:
Like Humpty Dumpty, Albert Collier was picked on.

13

A strangling wind, yes, his weight
Can still hold his own, wind-roughed
Down to his cracking trousers.
How could he fly or blow away?
A radio I've never had to operate.
A group with question marks doffed
Like school caps, rabble-rousers;
Questions they know I can't waive.
I wish I could abracadabra and create
Albert Collier: *We've had enough*
Albert, turn up, rise from your slumber,
A prank's a prank, you fooled us anyway.
My prayer or spell fuels a spate
Of overlapping shouts; voices-off
To a man splayed on the valley tundra
With a reply he'll never relay.

14

I silence them with a cry so hoarse
I don't recognise it, a shrill chord
Creeping in from nowhere I know.
Their looks reveal all their eyes' white
Like I'm Albert Collier's corpse,
Blue-faced, blank-eyed and slack-jawed.
Radio is what I said I'd do and radio
I will. *Oh scunt! Rass! Shites!*
The one fact fires from every synapse:
A cool gap, a weight loss, a fucking turd.
This can't be, every face knife-throws;
It can, if I'm to believe my C.N.S.
My radio might be in a copse
With Albert Collier, no longer bothered
By you and me is the look I let go.
A.C. and D.C. in their absence unite.

15

A unity few among us can bear.
We step as if shouldering the globe,
On stone I told them to check
In front as well as behind,
Placing their foot square.
A group suddenly depleted of anodes;
Fit to eat all the hill's chalk,
Tongue-tied and more than inclined
To lose what meagre will it has spare.
As we cross from slab to strobe-
Lighted slab on a bridge without bark
Or any kind of wood, cameras do not wind
On new film in that automatic wheeze, nor
Do camera-clicks race flashes and reload;
Not a pleased word, just requests
To retrace steps as if time can rewind.

16

What happened to Albert Collier
Occurred on that very peak; go back?
We're at the opening of forest
Able to shield us from a storm,
Destined to worsen according to the brier's
Sudden deep discolouring; my almanac.
Listen for the duffing of helicopter blades,
My failure to radio-in is an alarm;
When we hear that sound I'll fire
Flares I still have in my rucksack.
'It's impossible for them to locate us
Once we're buried in that mausoleum.'
I look at a face branded with panic brighter
Than any flare and decide not to attack
But pamper what little courage is left.
These flares can break a mature limb.

17

They can clear those treetop twigs
However tightly strung; if one's fucked
I've a spare. 'Why —' not another gripe —
'Cancel things at this late stage,
We've a good guide, we're men not kids.'
No; he's among the ones I'd clocked
By tagging his name to a stereotype,
Stored in a bone-bound book whose pages
Are cooled lava, molten and rapids
Rolled into one. I have his mug-shot
Demarcating certain features, like
Eyes that frisk you as if reading a gauge,
From the top of your head to the tip
Of your toe; eyes that turn you inside-out,
Zipping off to the next target ripe
For his very being to be savaged.

18

Names I latched onto personal details
(Learned from a correspondence course
Based on unlikely association),
Spring up like the numbers rung
On those preposterous old tills:
Jean-Pierre, broker at the Bourse,
He may be, his body, though, belongs
To a marine and his eyes are no nun's;
A high hawk's on a fieldmouse's tail.
I'm paranoid I inform my instinct, worse,
Unable to spot right from wrong;
Any moment my neck will be wrung.
I ask myself, can I honestly tell
I was told, *you're good*? Of course;
Maybe; we press deeper as light puts on
A green I failed to describe in the sun.

19

Language can stretch so far
Then it snaps, stinging the user:
Light must hit the eye to milk
Sense from the mind; experience
Showed me it. I could say this bar
Pierces a leaf for a leaf's colour;
That if I were to dash a noisy silk
Would tear (yes, here even silence
Is sound); that light is an avatar
Cradled and caressed to a cat's purr;
That light has a smell. I feel guilt
Well up as if I'd betrayed my province
All over again; my Shangri-La;
Like a fact passed on in a whisper
That ends up lying to the hilt.
My past is my conscience.

20

We've no choice, we must split
In two; half go on, half be patient.
The chopper bound for here will soon
Round Albert Collier peak and descend
So close you'll make out the pilot's
Eye-colour; razor-grass will lie obedient.
Which half will be referred to as baboons
To walk or not to have walked here end
To end, I leave to history; exhibit
One is Albert Collier, my first client
To go in this outsized, ice-made tomb.
Death never pays dividends. . . .
I'll do what I've worked out perfect
Over years: pack and clock some decent
Miles between me and a woken town
Wishing me dead; once a sleeping friend.

21

The stream again . . . we'd said farewell
To six, taking the path slung uppermost
Allowing for a flood. Consider
These banks, a tall man's leg-span,
Widened to twenty times that; dwell
On these clean rocks, smooth as amethyst
In the fleshy water – my alma mater –
Seen in the bed now like trepang;
Having to shoulder a tonne's-swell
Four-deep in hours. I recall this
Failure to cull belief, an atmosphere,
As I did my light-sermon on bitumen.
Trees we side-stepped up to the skull
In cloud along the chalk neck, have us
At their ankles. Leaves in strata
Laid over years climb high as stockings.

Leaves here are unlike the squirts
People shin through in a public park:
A fall that's so discrete children
Single out leaves to chase and catch
Before they lightly touch the earth.
Now these five I am burdened with start
Cursing the forest they paid rent
To journey; a leaf-and-mud-mix pack
Weighting boots worse than the hurt
Of jogging a few blocks. A good heart
Would revert to the tape these men
Breasted, beginning from scratch,
Bending for them as in the past. Revert?
I get a string of snide remarks,
As the branches tease and torture them,
About lying bumph that gave them the itch.

23

'One must admire the excellent trail.'
Straining for cries that were genuine
Not badgered, how was I to know when
To give up the lead and reconnoitre;
That by the next clearing two males
Would be gone; not fallen behind,
Thinner than the giddy oxygen
Breathed at the peak; the broker
And the post-graduate horticultural
Specialist near to blows swearing blind
The other came in last. I ordered them
To watch each other diving back on the
Trail, damning city types for too casual
An approach to this place, with no mind
For danger, until I found where the seven
Trails became five at a reef I remember.

24

Remembering how I ordered myself
As much as everyone to mind they step
On stone, not shrubbery that looked safe
Though overhanging in barefaced growth,
I saw the two still figures on a shelf
Of rock below, ignorant of each other, except
Both had caught an exact lack of grace.
How without so much as a cry? Why both?
I'd take too long climbing the cliff;
Its two hundred-foot drop would worry an adept.
What's plastered down there on each face?
A rotten look from men whose cut throats
My binoculars showed oozing their life.
I combed the bush length and breadth
For a struggle, weapon or any trace
Of a lost footing; not even a hoax.

25

On this trail all had to sidle,
Inching with their best foot forward,
On a beam-width that could throw
If the stare slackened or fixed
A stranglehold. Didn't they chuckle
When I said this on the asphalt road?
You can always blame the valley, for
Brewing mist ushered at you, a slick
In a slow tumble from irrevocable
Miles, driving the light backwards;
For the thinnest sunlit shower
Named Raining-whippet in my republic,
After those dogs you are able
To see through almost against a hard
Sun; for fine drizzles you know
Oiled the cobble from which a foot slips.

26

A polished leaf scraping every ounce
Of light remaindered in the gorge.
Whichever, we blame spirits, wraiths,
What appears not to flinch at anything;
What can camouflage the best evidence,
A botanist or broker's lie, and absorb
These three uncalled-for deaths.
Back to the four in that clearing
Saving three from a fourth, facing once
And for all my assassin. (I ask God
To spare those three, my solitary oath.)
I know, by the way he relishes leaving
Me last – his first mistake – he's convinced
I'll come to him, like the hungry dog
In a leaf can wring from the earth
The last light that is its bone.

27

Valley and forest, river and mountain
I know as guide, making strange the more
I stare, discard your impartial air.
I return, boots caked in leaves and mud,
Never too heavy for me, to that clearing
Of clearings where witnesses, if they are
Alive, joke or argue with a man they fear
Or trust. If I need my walk to bounce proud
It's now. Dead leaves were a sponge or spring
That threw back my step. Now they kill my soar,
Dragging at my heel, stretching as if to tear
My tendon. Light in here, quiet or loud,
Hardens as the yards between us close in,
To battalions, sided with him as never before;
Light I've seen play on water or swing clear
In a chute sunk through trees from cloud.

28

When I first entered this forest,
A vulture flew over, I was cursed.
Later, I bumped into a big nest,
It was the same bird, I was its guest.

I'd found a home left for good,
No eggs, no warm feathers, no food;
A webbing of twigs balanced on a rod
And a tangible absence in the whole wood.

It flew deeper in then disappeared
Into branches with vines like beards;
Suddenly a wing-beat filled the place
As it broke cover in a dive for my face.

The last thing I saw shone in its eye
Burning a hole in the earth and the sky;
Not me and the backdrop in which I'm to die,
Or me curling-up my forearms flicked high;

Not even a wide mouth drying up the forest air,
Nor all the eyes' white peeled eyelids can bare;
Not a single leaf, vine or drop of water,
Just a beast staring back at me and me not there.

29

I came round thrashing at what I took for bars,
Taller than any tree, high as the stars;
My blows caught so many it was slaughter;
As I cut through one clean, it made another.

How long did I fight before I came to see
What I faced was not an enemy,
Not the man contracted to destroy me,
Nor the shadows conscripted in his army?

I was soaked, my breath gone, my heartbeat
Multiplied back to one, I was butcher's meat.
This forest and all in it pissed on me:
How the stream sounded close to glee.

My prison without windows and doors;
My enemy stuck in my very pores;
The bars that X-ray me down to my bones;
The light loved without knowing why I love.

30

From a tree's trunk lava erupts;
Cools where the bark emerges
From itself; a clenched fist;
An asleep child.
                 Air becomes soil
For the plaited roots, shaken out,
Having shook itself free from earth;
Earth it now tries to net.

They might rise up to stockade him,
Or loosen into boneless whips and reel
His ankles, wrists, neck; struggle
Tightens them, slackening when his muscles
Take on a sail's slack.

                  Rass!
The blasted vine grab my foot,
My cutlass blade bounce off,
Vine, vine, vine, I used to twist,
Use as twine.
              The man out there
To kill me must be near to God
Or Devil. Who to pray to?
Who curse?

Postscript

If you come to a clearing and there are women,
Leggy women, nursing champagne glass stems,
Stave any surprise; your assassin is a master
Of limited disguise; even a man of his calibre
Could not make it to this unqualified spot
Not on any regional map in a time to laugh at.

You wish it was him then at least you'd know:
This brings the driest forest twig to your sole –
Gunfire from a pressurised carton
Stamped by a child in a square of pigeons;
Heads turn as towards a guest whose knock
On returning from a steamed car got lost.

You straighten, breathe deep and flash the smile
For all border situations meant to lower the aim
Of rifles trained on you to bitumen that can take it.
A raised glass gathering every last drop of light
In the forest is ignored as you cross the borderland.
You know from the soft green you have re-entered

The atmosphere you love. A table overturns. The chink
When ice bobs in a light drink is a crash,
A half-full or half-empty bottle's muted pop
And the chase with you as hare and six bitches
For bloodhounds begins; one man has laid odds
That you will be theirs inside a mile, you answer him

With expletives and a sign that can never be official
In wartime or peacetime, and wind forced out.
Barks announce dawn and a dying night you clocked
On your feet and will carry under your eyes
For the calendar, remaindered, that is your life;
You wouldn't wish it on a dog, never mind anyone.